THE ROCK

THE ROCK

An Outline of Ecclesiastical History

*From the Caesars to the
Great Occidental Schism*

E. M. SCHORB, SR.

HILL HOUSE   **NEW YORK**

*There is nothing more serious than the sacri-
lege of schism because there is no just cause
for severing the unity of the Church.*
                              —Saint Augustine

*Schisms do not originate in a love of truth,
which is a source of courtesy and gentleness,
but rather in an inordinate desire for suprem-
acy.*
                              —Baruch Spinoza

As the dawn of the first century spread its rays of light upon the pageantry of Roman history, it beheld events that were destined by far to produce a mightier influence upon posterity than anything that had ever transpired in the previous history of the world.

At that great period we find Augustus, the first emperor of Rome, with a standing army of three hundred and forty thousand men, a Senate of his choice, the populace contented with free food and games furnished by the state. The Empire which started previous to Augustus as the City of Rome, now extended from the Atlantic to the Euphrates three thousand miles in distance, and from the Danube to the English Channel. It was later to extend also from Scotland to the floodgates of the Nile and the African Desert, with a population of approximately one hundred million.

If the reader will glance back over the pages of Roman history, from the time of the founding of the city, and carry himself up to the present period, he will upon analyses discover the most noteworthy fact for all intents and purposes of this outline, to be that, during the entire history of Rome, conquests were being carried on which amalgamated peoples who were not only primitive and nomadic but of diametrically different thought from various and sundry geographical locations, from the torrid heat of the tropics to the colder countries of the North. In view of the probable fact that the peoples of the so-called colonies possessed a certain amount of loyalty for their erstwhile leaders, which among all people and in all communities spring up and succeed in leading the majority, there can be no doubt but that subjugation by a power hundreds or thousands of miles distant was not altogether agreeable. Therefore the thing that always happens in a case of that kind occurred. A wise statesman appeared upon the horizon, just previous to the dictatorship of Augustus. A great soldier, politician and a man of letters, Julius Caesar. Caesar realized that the Empire could no longer be ruled by a few politicians from Rome, and by virtue of that fact brought the city to be regarded as a capital instead of mistress over all dominions. He gave full citizenship to all the Transpadine Gauls and to various sections in Transalpine Gaul and to other colonies.

During and contemporary with the Augustan period, materialism ran rampart. The philosophers, who were the leaders of thought, had a vague idea of unity or a form of brotherhood of man based upon the old paganistic idea. The masses, however, were as lost sheep in search of some religious thought. The glory of empire destroyed even the old beliefs to such an extent that many were consolidating the various heathenistic rites into a new religious order.

As though predestined, an event occurred just at that time that was not only to fill the spiritual void of the masses, but to revolutionize the entire order of affairs, not so much, however, for the existent generations as for succeeding ones and for those to come, so long as the present civilization remains upon earth.

Four years before the beginning of our present calendar Jesus was born. While the Jews were the only believers, up to that time, in the one God infinite and had been promised in the Old Testament a Messiah, they believed and could not estrange themselves from the thought of an earthly king and deliverer.

Jesus proclaimed himself as a Messiah and founder of a kingdom "not of this world", a brotherhood of man, mankind being the children of God; his spiritual powers being demonstrated by marvelous works and mercy. His messages were delivered with authority, but with great compassion for the poor and downtrodden. He had nothing but the greatest contempt and scorn for the Pharisees, a Jewish religious party, that insisted upon the strict observance of the law, and who were the most ardent believers in an earthly king, who would deliver them from foreign domination. He scorned the Pharisees for their hypocrisy, assumed sanctity, and their traditional ideas. While the teachings of Jesus dwelt upon the spiritual side of the affairs of man, inculcating into their minds and hearts, the spirit of love and compassion, for one another, and for the poor and the lowly in spirit, and those bereft of health; his condemnation came down heavily upon the heads of those men of wealth in Palestine.

In addition to the many messages of Jesus, and the parables, he reversed some of the laws of Moses, by which the Jews had lived from times immemorial. Where the Mosaic law brought vengeance down upon the head of an offender, Christ taught the doctrine of love and compassion toward the enemy of an individual, or the law. He referred to the Mosaic law as the old order, and his teachings as the new order.

The doctrine that Jesus taught, while in the succeeding centuries, has swayed nations of the western world, left its imprint upon the so-called heathen nations of the eastern world, and to a certain degree has revolutionized the economic forces of the world, was at the time considered revolutionary. His denunciation of the rich, his contempt for the Pharisees, his rejection of an earthly kingship, or anything of a material nature, and the natural inability of the leaders of thought of the time, to grasp the greatness of the doctrine, nor the power that lay behind it, created an agitation for his crucifixion. He was accused of heterodoxy and blasphemy before the Jewish Sanhedrin, was brought before Pontius Pilate, the Roman procurator (26-36), who consented to his death, because of his acceptance of the title "king", which was reserved for Caesar, and was used against Jesus, by those whom he denounced, and who made the liberal interpretation of treason from it. Jesus was crucified by authority of the Roman law, in far away Judea, by the Rome that needed his message so urgently during the Augustan period, and which inherited and profited so much through it.

As was the birth of Jesus predestined to occur at a time that the world of that period needed a spiritual balance wheel, so it seemed preordained that Rome was to be the spiritual power-house of the world, through which Christ's messages, were to be sent to the remotest ends of the earth. Jesus' reversal of that law of Moses, calling for an eye for an eye, and a tooth for a tooth, and instructing his brethren, that if a man slap thee once on one cheek, to turn to him the other, was best exemplified by him, upon the cross, when he said, "Father forgive them, for they know not what they do."

The next epochal step which was an important link in the chain of events, that was to have an everlasting effect upon civilization, was the conversion of the Pharisee Paul, his gospels, epistles, and missions.

Paul, as a Pharisee, persecuted Christians, but by another one of those strange turns of events, it was this persecutor of Christians, whose preaching of the Christian doctrine, and whose migrations into Asia, Macedonia, Greece, and Illyricum, where he founded churches, who planted the seed of Christianity, the seed that grew, in idolatrous Rome. Paul was imprisoned in Rome while his small band of followers worshipped secretly. In the year 67 Paul was put to death by Nero, in Rome. His fearless spirit, the fact that his persecutors were always met with prayer for forgiveness, and for their enlightenment, plus the fact that Paul died a martyr, without doubt had its reaction favorable to his teachings on Christianity. However, it was to be two hundred and fifty years later that Christianity was to supplant Heathenism.

During the interim an immense amount of blood was shed by the ever growing bands of Christians who never ceased to be persecuted by the fanatical followers of the old thought. Emperors came, one after another, endeavoring to hold the Empire together by force: first by right of family succession, then appointed by the army. Augustus said that he found Rome a city of brick, and left it of marble. During those two

hundred and fifty years Rome degener-
ated from marble to a moral clay. To be
sure the marble remained, and in the
declining days of heathenism cities
were wealthy, municipal improve-
ments were being made on a large
scale, and subject countries were being
impregnated by Roman culture. However there was a growing sensuality,
slave-holding became general in middle class households, and theatrical
performances became licentious and
unchaste.

After a bitter and bloody struggle internal war with Licinius, Constantine became sole master of the Roman Empire
(306-337).

Wars, internal and external, atheism,
religious persecution, and last but not
least, imperial glory, attendant by
moral decay, had brought about the
weakening of the underlying strata of
the Empire to the extent that its imperial star was in the descendent. Before
its star was to go below the horizon,
however, another great link in the
never-ending chain which is to lead
into the centuries, so long as civiliza-

tion remains, or so long as any records of the present civilization remain, to be passed on to another.

From the time of Trajan (98-117), Christianity was an illegal religion. In spite of systematic persecutions, brought on by the various Emperors and advocated by the conservative Romans of the time who believed the old Heathen religion was indispensable to the unity of the Empire, Christianity was slowly but surely gaining a foothold. The last of the great persecutions of Christians was ordered by Diocletian. By comparison, all previous attempts to stamp out Christianity were insignificant. Terrible sufferings were inflicted, without success, on the part of the Emperor. Diocletian, for reasons of his own, abdicated, which abdication was followed by civil wars culminating in Constantine becoming the Emperor.

Just before his decisive battle and victory over Licinius, known as the battle of Milvian Bridge, Constantine thought he saw a vision of the cross, with words over the Cross to the effect, "in this sign thou shalt conquer". The conversion of Constantine was very gradual, but more and more he depended upon prayer to lead him to victory in battles. His vision and victory culminated in his acceptance of Christianity, which made it the predominating religion. Constantine granted freedom of open worship to the now larger bodies of Christians, which very quickly gave birth to the organized Christian Church.

As we go through the pages of Roman history, from the time of Augustus, we perceive the building of a spiritual Empire or the Kingdom of which Jesus spoke, within an Empire. Constantine sanctioned the Christian doctrine and made it lawful for its adherents to worship and preach openly. However, the Church started with the preaching of Peter and Paul. That was known as the apostolic age of the Church. Small societies were organized along the line of small republics. They were guided by a body of elders or bishops and a body of deacons, the members choosing their officers and lending a voice in ecclesiastical affairs. In the second century we find the bishops over the elders, with the office of bishop growing in importance as the number of followers increased and the line of demarcation between laity and the clergy becomes more noticeable.

Soon we find the bishop of the city church taking superintendence over the adjacent country churches. At the close of the second century we find the church conceived of as a unity, under the leadership of bishops, in connection with the apostolic sees, or the churches founded by the apostles in person. As the apostles recognized Peter as their head, the bishops of Rome were recognized by their contemporaries as the successors of Peter, and therefore took precedence over all other bishops. Rome's historic relation to Peter and Paul, its grandeur, plus the strength of the church there, gave to the Roman See preeminence and to the city the seat of Church government. During the period from Augustus to Constantine we have visualized the amalgamation of many peoples of various tongues into an Empire, the nucleus of which having been inspired by a certain amount of freedom, or to put it another way, without undue oppression, and by virtue of the proverb, "necessity being the mother of invention", hard and productive work. As a result of the driving force of the early inhabitants, Rome was crowned with Imperial glory attended by wealth which lead on to slave-holding on a large scale, and many other luxuries hitherto unknown. The natural result of all the circumstances or conditions, one leading to another, was moral decay. However, while those conditions prevailed and had their culmination on the material side of the Empire, that side that was forcibly put together by the military and held together by the strong arm of the Emperors through the army, the so-called fall of the Roman Empire spelled continuity of its influence upon the world.

As we lead into the era of transition in the fourth century and travel through the middle ages to the fifteenth century, we see history repeating itself on the side of force, conquest and materialism. Contrasted with that, we see the great Kingdom of Christ on the spiritual side, continually gaining momentum, becoming a greater unity and lending its great unseen power whenever and wherever it would help the oppressed or bring about the idea of individual freedom. True it was that, at various times, as certain individuals in the high clergy acquired power, the human element within them gained the upper hand which labeled them with greed and licentiousness. That, however, is a minute detail and hardly worth recording, inasmuch as it does not deal with the great spirit of Jesus and its tremendous effect upon mankind.

During the Mediaeval period we find the conquering Germanic nations intermingling with the peoples who previously made up the Roman Empire. While the Teutonic tribes influenced society, Roman civilization reacted on them. Civilization was bestowed upon the conquerors by the conquered. The sole bond of unity was the Christian Church which not only educated the conquerors but guided them, both in religious and civil affairs. Civil government was in chaos, but out of that chaos Christendom alone, made up of various and sundry peoples and tongues, was the only unity.

During the middle ages Pontifical authority reached its full stature and, while Ecclesiastical and Civil authority clashed frequently for authority, the fundamental causes were no doubt attributable to the ingrained human weaknesses which we often discover when one element disagrees with another as to policy, plus the element of greed and the lack of the spiritual or application of the spiritual law.

Circa 570 another event occurred which was to have a tremendous influence upon the world of political intercourse. Mohammed was born and early left an orphan. He believed himself divinely inspired, became a prophet and imparted to his followers a doctrine. Whether his doctrine was borrowed from Christ and the Jewish religion with which he became acquainted through his trips into Palestine and Syria, where he no doubt came into contact with monks and rabbis, is immaterial because the fact remains that his influence was to add to the shaking up of the then civilization on a larger scale than hitherto.

Not only northern Africa and Asia Minor came under the influence of the Koran, but Christian Europe was seriously threatened. Early in the eighth century the Saracens opened their campaign for the conquest of Spain. They were successful to the degree, that in 720 they stood north of the Pyrenees and were checked by the valiant Frank infantry.

While Mohammed and his successors were writing their way into history, the Germanic nation and the Christian Church were coming into close cohesion. Karl the Great, or Charlemagne, whom we see as a foremost conqueror and ruler, a German in blood and speech, became king of the Franks in 771. After many years of bitter struggle, he conquered the Saxons and forced Christianity upon them. In 772 he was summoned to Rome by Pope Hadrian I to protect him from the attacks of the Lombards, with whom Charlemagne was at enmity, though he had married and divorced a daughter of the Lombard king. Desiderius, the Lombard king, demanded the Pope to anoint the sons of Carloman (Charlemagne's brother) as kings of the Franks. Charlemagne crossed the Alps in 772, captured Desiderius and made him a prisoner in a Frank monastery and himself became king of Lombard and master of Italy.

Empress Irene was on the throne of the Byzantine empire which was regarded as the eastern Roman Empire which, at that period, rendered little or no protection to Rome. The time being opportune to throw off the Byzantine rule, Charlemagne, who was on another visit to Italy, was crowned Emperor of Rome on Christmas Day in the year 800 by Pope Leo III. The coronation took place in the Basilica of St. Peter during the celebration of mass, amid the acclamation of the people. Thus a German became the successor of the Caesars Augustus and Constantine.

Ireland had been converted to Christianity during the middle of the fifth century. During the seventh and eighth centuries, previous to which Ireland had sent missions into Scotland; there came Saxon missionaries from England, the most eminent of which was Winfred who converted the Hessians and founded monasteries among them. The wilderness was reclaimed by the energy of four thousand monks and brought into a state of cultivation under the disciple of Winfred, Sturm.

Other German tribes became peaceful converts and, under the direction of the popes, the German Church was organized, about 747. In 801 the Scandinavians were converted by the efforts of Ansgar who held the archbishopric of Hamburg with papal consent, which was later transferred to Bremen 849, after Hamburg had been plundered by pirates. Ansgar succeeded in the conversion of Denmark, Sweden and, after much resistance, in Norway.

From the death of Charlemagne we see his empire dissolve through dissention between his descendants and the lack of strength on the part of any one of them to dominate. There also arose a nationalistic spirit among the various tongues comprising the Empire. We witness the rise of the kingdoms of France, Germany and Italy. These nations became the prey of the northern nomads, known as the Northmen, who sacked their cities, robbed and murdered as the Saracens were doing in the south. However, there was one great difference in the final outcome in the north. In France the Northmen were finally ceded land as the price of peace. The main or most noteworthy characteristic of the Northmen was their adaptability to become standard bearers of the nationality of their adoption.

Rolf, or Rollo, one of the most formidable chiefs of the Northmen, accepted lands (911) in the district later known as Normandy, received baptism, received the title of Duke, and loyally served King Charles. Norman help brought about the rank of kingdom for France, which had formally been been a duchy, thus making Hugh Capet the founder of French sovereigns.

During that period, and up until many centuries later, we find nationalities moving and shifting about Europe, comparable with a checker player moving his checkers about the board. The shifting is attended by the mixture of bloods, thus absorbing any and all racial characteristics that may have been present. During that period of nomadism at sea the Northmen discovered Iceland and Greenland. Iceland was settled by them in 874 and in about the year 1100 a colony was planted at Greenland. It is also believed that Vinland, which they discovered, was the mainland of the coast of New England. Like all other paradoxical events in history, while the Northmen pillaged and were outlaws, the world has much to thank them for and their influence and resourcefulness would be very much missed were they never to have taken their place in history.

Under Otto I, a German king who, as Charlemagne previously had done, turned his eyes again toward Italy which had been in a state of anarchy since 896, or since the departure of the Carlovingian emperor. About 925 profligacy was rampant both among the Romans and the Pontiffs, making unity impossible. First as an act of knightly virtue, Otto came down into Italy, saved the beautiful Adelheid, widow of the previous king and imprisoned by Berengar, Italian king who wanted her to marry his son. Otto forced the Italian king to recognize him as his master, and married the young queen. He assumed the imperial office and was crowned by Pope John XII in St. Peter's in 962. Later Otto caused John to be deposed for various crimes and made Leo VIII his successor. While Otto was absent John returned and Leo was driven out. John soon after died, whereupon the Romans elected Benedict. Otto was to return the third time to abolish the factions who had so long degraded the Church and Rome. Otto acquired the southern extremity of Italy through having arranged a marriage between his son and a Greek princess by name Theophano. The aforesaid events led up to the formation of what was known as The Holy Roman Empire.

The Holy Roman Empire was an undivided community under the Pope and Emperor. They were the heaven appointed spiritual and secular heads.

From the political standpoint it was a combination under one sovereignty of Germany and Italy.

This political union reached its height during the reign of Henry III (1039-1056). One of the most notable events, which took place during the reign of Henry III, was the bringing about of the "Truce of God", which was originated by the bishops in 1041, and favored by him. The decree ordered that no private feuds should be prosecuted between sunset of Wednesday and sunrise Monday or that period covered by the most sacred events in the life of Jesus. In those dark and troublous times it is very significant that the influence of Christianity was to bring itself to the fore so strongly. For those who could not defend themselves against violence, the edict was especially welcome.

While "The Holy Roman Empire" was to have been interpreted as a joint community, under the authority of the Pope and Emperor, there were continual clashes of authority between the secular and spiritual heads. In the absence

of anything bordering upon constitu-
tionalism, harmony was dependent
upon the respective characteristics of
the Emperors and Popes as they appeared upon the horizon of their respective authorities. Thus, during the
reign of Henry III, more authority was
assumed by the secular head. So it
happened that when Henry IV became
the sovereign and attempted to rule not
only the Empire but the Church, he en-
countered an exceptionally strong man
to deal with in the celebrated Hildebrand, or Gregory VII.

Hildebrand, the son of a carpenter, was
born in Tuscany in 1018. He received
his education in a monastery in Rome
and spent some time in the great monastery of Cluny in France. He became
an influential adviser of the Popes.
During that period priests were indulg-
ing in marriage on a large scale, thus
violating the old Church law of celi-
bacy. The sale of ecclesiastical rights
was also being conducted on a large
scale. Another matter that caused great
friction was the investure upon the ecclesiastics by the kings. Hildebrand
who, for twenty-four years previous to

his elevation as spiritual head of the church, had wielded a paramount influence both in government and as a confidential adviser of several preceding Popes, appears as a divinely dispatched messenger to restore order from chaos and make more clear the line of demarcation between Church and State.

In 1073 Hildebrand became Pope. As Pope he was known as Gregory II. The avowed object of his reign was to abolish investiture of the Clergy, by the Laity or the counselors of the German monarch who were selling ecclesiastical benefices to the highest bidders and the practice, which had become quite general, of marriage by Priests. His secondary purpose was to deliver bishops and abbots from all feudal service.

Thus we find at this period two powerful influences diametrically opposed, one with a strictly spiritual trend of thought and purpose in view, the other possessing a material thought and ultimate purpose; each for a time vainly endeavoring to conquer the other; one using spiritual methods, the other using force.   Henry IV was   repeatedly excommunicated and decreed no longer to be Emperor, and at one time waited at Gregory's gates three days in penitential garb begging absolution from excommunication, which he received, only to violate his promises and to be again excommunicated. Gregory, on the other hand, was by Monarchical decree, declared deposed as Pope by Henry. Gregory died in exile after Henry succeeded in taking possession of Saint Peter's in Rome and the elevation of the excommunicated Archbishop Guibert of Ravenna to the Papacy. Gregory's last words were, "I have loved justice and hated iniquity, and therefore do I die in exile."

As we view the never-ending drama of history, Hildebrand was one of those immortals who are constantly predestined to appear in our midst at a time when most needed and whose avowed purpose becomes an accomplishment in succeeding generations and sometimes centuries. Their greatness can only be measured by posterity which only can see the imprint of their good works by virtue of the civil and spiritual order by which they are surrounded and live under. To ever improve that good order, such messengers as Hildebrand and many others have appeared predestined.

As a result of the work of Gregory the faith and confidence of nations were strengthened, society was safeguarded from the danger of Church offices becoming hereditary and from the formation of a priestly caste. While these do not appear to be great reforms to the casual thinker accustomed to present day environment, if one will reflect a bit further, carry oneself back to the period then think of what the effect would be on present day life and politics had they not taken place, one can easily understand why the name of Hildebrand occupies a place among the immortals.

During the interim from 1096-1270, events were taking place that were causing a great blood sacrifice on the part of Christian nations, which was later to be off-set by many benefits in the nature of an advanced civilization.

During the earliest ages of the Church pilgrimages were made to the Holy

Land by Christians to visit the locali-
ties that had been hallowed by Jesus.
In the tenth century these pilgrimages
multiplied very rapidly as a result of an
opinion that the end of the world was
at hand. This opinion was accepted by
some to the extent that they sold their
estates and emigrated to Palestine to
await the second coming.

In the seventh century, when Jerusalem
was taken from Christian possession,
the pilgrimages were tolerated and, on
account of the financial profit to those
in possession, were to an extent welcome. In 969 the Egyptian Sultans became masters of Jerusalem, at which
time a decided change took place in the
treatment of Christians. In 1010 a persecution of Christians took place on a
large scale when Christian Temples in
Jerusalem and the neighborhood were
destroyed. In 1073 another persecution by the Turks took place. Native
Christians, as well as Pilgrims, were
oppressed and subjected to great indignities. The persecutions very naturally
had a great reaction in Europe. Mohammedans, who were the constant
and dangerous enemies of Christian

Europe, as evidenced by the fact that in 720 they stood north of the Pyrenees with Spain in their possession, succeeded by additional overt acts of Christian persecution in Palestine, in uniting Europe against them.

Seven crusades were launched by Christian Europe and Asia against the Mohammedans, some greater than others. In addition to the seven, there was one known as the Children's Crusade. The latter was the result of a misinterpretation of the injunction of Jesus to let the little children come to him.

Previous to the first crusade undisciplined bands numbering two hundred thousand of both sexes, in their ardor and passion inspired by the preaching of Peter the Hermit, started for Constantinople. Due to disorganization they were obliged to separate. All perished except about seven thousand and these perished in Asia Minor, their bones being found by the second expedition, known better as the first Crusade.

While none of the sovereigns took part in the first Crusade, their vassals and the lesser nobility took part with great earnestness and devotion to the cause. A stately army consisting of five hundred thousand men, set out for Asia Minor. In 1099, after many victories, Jerusalem fell to the Crusaders and became the capital of a new kingdom. Unfortunately the spirit of the Cross, which was the symbol of the Crusaders, did not prevail upon the occasion of the great success. Ten thousand Arabs were slaughtered and Jews were burned in synagogues to which they had fled. The new kingdom lasted until 1187, when Jerusalem was captured by Saladin.

At the insistence of the Pope, St. Bernard preached for a second Crusade. Conrad III of Germany and Louis VII of France assumed the leadership and set out with imposing armies for Palestine in 1147. Both Monarchs reached Palestine with shattered forces, most of their armies having been destroyed by the Turks. Greek double-dealing and immorality on the part of the Crusaders are blamed for the disastrous failure of the second Crusade. The purpose of the second Crusade was to recapture Edessa, which was regarded as the bulwark of the Kingdom of Jerusalem which had been taken and destroyed by the Sultan Zenki of Mosel.

After the capture of Jerusalem, which ended the new kingdom of the Christians, by Saladin, Europe was fired anew with the spirit of the Crusade. In the year 1189 a third Crusade was launched under the leadership of Frederick Barbarossa of Germany, Philip Augustus of France, Richard Coeur-de-Lion of England and William of Sicily, who were the most powerful monarchs of the West.

The German Emperor defeated the Turks in several battles, but was drowned in the midst of his victorious career. His army proceeded to Palestine and, with the help of the French and English forces, captured Acre in 1191. Quarrels between the English and French Kings ensued, followed by dissention in the ranks of the Crusaders, which caused the armies to return home.

In 1202 the Fourth Crusade was undertaken for the conquest of the infidels, under the direction of French barons. The effort was an utter failure. Arrived at Venice and not being able to satisfy the Venetians from a mercenary standpoint they were, much to the displeasure of the Pope, diverted by assisting the Venetians in the capture of Zara which had been wrested from them by the king of Hungary, after which they accompanied the Venetian fleet to Constantinople which resulted in the pillage of that city and the establishment of the Latin Empire under Count Baldwin of Flanders which was later (1261) put an end to by Michael Palaiologus, head of a Greek Empire at Nicaea. The Fourth Crusade ended in 1204.

In the year 1212 many thousands of French and German children were organized and sent out in two distinct expeditions to Marseilles and Italian seaports to be conveyed to the Holy Land. That Fifth (or Children's) Crusade, as mentioned earlier, was generally predicated upon the misconstruction of the injunction of Christ to let little children come to him. Many of those who did not perish on the way were carried off to the slave markets. A very few, however, did succeed in returning.

Two additional crusades were undertaken under the leadership of Louis IX of France. The first one (1248-1254) succeeded in capturing Damietta in Egypt (1249). The next year, however, Louis with his whole army was captured and was released only after much delay, the surrender of his conquests and the payment of a large ransom. Inspired by his great devotion, his honesty of purpose, the pious king led another Crusade. In 1270 he reached Tunis where he and most of his army perished from sickness.

Acre, the last town held by the Christians, fell to the Egyptian Mamelukes in 1291. Thus ended the Crusades.

The Crusades most decidedly were an epochal part of the history of the Middle Ages which were, as is obvious, a counterpart of the present and future, insofar as the closer amalgamation of peoples and the knitting together of trade were concerned. To quote a celebrated writer of history, the net effects of the Crusades were: "First, it is true that the conquests made in the East were all surrendered. The Holy places were given up. Yet the Turks had received a check which was a protection to Europe during the period when its monarchies were forming and were gaining in force to encounter them anew and repel their dangerous aggressions. Second, the Feudal system of Europe was smitten with a mortal blow. Smaller fiefs, either by sale or by the death of the holders, were swallowed up in the larger. The anarchical spirit was counteracted. Political unity was promoted. Third, there was a lessening of the social distance between suzerain and serf. They fought side by side and aided one another in common perils. The consequence was an increase of sympathy. Fourth, there was an expansion of knowledge. There was a widening of geographical knowledge. An acquaintance was gained with other peoples and countries. To the more civilized Saracens the Crusaders seemed cruel and barbarous.

The Crusaders in turn were impressed with the superior advancement and elegance of the Saracens. It was not the lord only who beheld distant lands, the serf was taken from the soil to which he had been tied. He drew stimulus and information from sojourning under other skies. Fifth, a great impulse was given to trade and commerce. An acquaintance was gained with new products, natural and artificial. New wants were created. Sixth, the cities advanced in strength and wealth. Important social consequences resulted from their growth."

As a matter of recording the reaction of nations, which will be referred to again in this volume, and which is the only element upon which to base a prognostication of the future of nations, it will be well to quote the same historian as to why the Crusades ended: "(1) The absence of novelty in such undertakings; (2) the long experience of hardships belonging to them, which tended to dampen the romantic zeal that had formed part of the motive; (3) the disappointments following upon the practical failure of so prodigious and costly exertions; (4) an altered condition of public feeling of a more general character. Antipathy to the infidel, the more exclusive sway of religious sentiment, were giving way to a mingling of secular aims and interests. There were new and wider fields of activity at home. The mood of men's minds was no longer the same."

While Christian Europe was spending its ardor preaching and executing the Crusades, thereby adding a link to the ever interlocking religious and political history of the civilization, an event took place in England which was destined to be the most far-reaching development, insofar as government and individual representation therein is concerned, than anything up to that time on record.

In the name of taxation King John of England robbed and coerced his subjects, especially the rich landowners and the Jews. After a dispute between the monks of Canterbury and John as regards the appointment of an archbishop, the Pope disregarding both appointed and made the monks elect a learned Englishman—Stephen Langton. John refused to recognize the election and drove the monks out of Canterbury. After having been excommunicated, England was placed under an interdict. John paid no heed to those measures, whereupon Pope Innocent III absolved his subjects from their allegiance and turned his Kingdom over to the king of France (1212).

Having lost the support of his people on account of his tyranny and licentiousness and threatened by invitation by Philip Augustus of France, who had called upon him to explain the murder of Arthur Duke of Brittany, his nephew, John was compelled to make his peace with the Pope. The Pope returned to him the Kingdom of England and Ireland, after he placed his crown at the feet of Pandulph, the Pope's legate, and submitted himself as the Pope's vassal. It was also agreed that a yearly rent should be paid to Rome by the King of England and his heirs forever.

Thus the dispute that brought about the election of Stephen Langton to the rank of Archbishop of Canterbury and the humility of John led to the great reform known as the Magna Carta.

Langton, a man of great vision, and the English Church united with the barons, demanded and received from King John, in the meadow of Runnymede situated on an island in the Thames, the Great Charter, which was the beginning of English constitutional Liberty, in the year 1215.

The Great Charter embodied the following: It recognized the rights of the Church, secured person and property from seizure and spoilation without the judgment of peers or the law of the land. There were regulations for courts of law. The benefits granted to the vassal were extended to the lower tenants. A great council to be formed and how it was to be convened was defined. "Liberties and free customs" of London and other towns were secured. Protection was given against oppressive exactions of the crown. The safety of merchants against exactions of in coming into and going out of, or in travelling through England was guaranteed. Even the criminal was given protection at law.

In the thirteenth century we see the rise and growth of cities; the origin of Municipal freedom, the two classes of cities; the effect of the early Roman Law; the beginning of trade and commerce on a fairly large scale; the Jewish money lenders who were the first to employ bills of exchange; the hazards of trade due to lack of respect for property rights on the sea; the recognition of the right of popular outbreak against bad government about which Guizot said "was the great guarantee for good government"; the rise of universities; the papal authority at its height; the spread of Mendicant Orders which attracted young men of talents and vigorous minds; Scholastic Theology, the teachers of which used Aristotle for their philosophical writings and Augustine for their theological writings; and the beginning of literature which heretofore had been confined to the monasteries along with most intellectual activity.

To sum up all of these developments briefly, we see a new class coming into being. While heretofore there were two classes in the cities vested with rights, we see the rise of the Burgher class, who by virtue of their increased intelligence asserted their rights. Under the older feudal system only two classes presented themselves to view, the clergy and the nobility on the one hand and the serfs on the other. The growth of cities was brought about by increased intelligence and the development of trade which followed the Crusades. The old Roman Law was revised, which not only assisted the lower classes to obtain more freedom, but also led to the right of inheritance. As a result of the Crusades trade routes were extended from the North Sea to the Mediterranean, thence to India and China. England exchanged sheep with Spain for horses. Cloths were traded for glass, etc. The Crusades having created a demand on the part of the West for Eastern products, the West in turn introduced their wares to the East. The Jews were persecuted in Europe for accepting interest on money loaned, while the Christians refused interest. Cities were chartered by the king in many instances and were in a distinct class from those under lords. Trade had its many hazards, due chiefly to shipwreck and diversity of coins. A certain noble in Brittany, pointing to a rock on which many vessels had been wrecked said, "I have a rock there more precious than the diamonds on the crown of a king." Whatever was cast upon the shore was considered the property of the neighboring lord. Insofar as the coinage system was concerned, in every fief it was necessary to change one's money and always at a loss. Under Louis IX only the king's coinage was good everywhere, the eighty lords who had the right of coinage must according to edict keep it within their respective territories.

In the era of 1270-1453 many events are taking place, the most important of which is the individualistic trend of nations, the populations becoming strongly animated with a nationalistic spirit, the influence of the old Roman Law upon government and the Church,

the Hundred Years War and the fall of
Constantinople to the Turks.

After a three year war with Edward I of
England, Philip IV of France found it
expedient to find new sources of reve-
nue. With that purpose in view he
practiced extortion upon the Jews and
to use the modern phrase, inflated the
money system, and levied unreasona-
ble taxes upon his subjects in general.
He also resolved to tax church property. The latter resolution brought him
into serious controversy with Pope
Boniface VIII who held his papal pre-
rogative as inviolate, as formerly did
Hildebrand. It was this controversy
that first brought about the clash of one
set of laws against another set. Philip
IV had been styled the King of Legists.
By these lawyers, or legists, who had
delved deeply into the Roman Law,
and who made interpretation thereof,
he was equipped with a weapon with
which to meet Pope or baron. In that
dispute of the right of taxation of
church properties Philip stood firmly
upon the Roman Law, the Pope upon
Canon Law which had long been gaining in power in Europe. In an edict, or

what is known as a Papal Bull, Boniface VIII forbade the imposition of extraordinary taxes upon the clergy without the consent of the Holy See. Philip responded by driving out of the country Roman priests through the issuance of an order forbidding foreigners to sojourn in France. At the same time he cut off contributions to Rome through an order forbidding money to be carried out of France. After a short reconciliation, Philip arrested a legate of the Pope which was followed by the summons of the French clergy to Rome for the purpose of settling the differences in France. Philip appealed to the nation. In April 1302 a body which, for the first time in history, was assembled in the Church of Notre Dame at Paris. The council contained deputies of universities and of towns, and is recognized as the first meeting of the States General in France. Philip was excommunicated and the Pope was preparing to depose him and to hand his kingdom over to Emperor Albert I.

The States General was reconvened in 1303. It was proposed by the legists that Philip convoke a general council of the Church, and to summon the Pope before it. William of Nogaret, the leading lawyer of the day, in the service of the king was directed to serve the notice on the Pope and to publish it in Rome. Nogaret was attended by a great enemy of the Pope and by several hundred hired soldiers. It is said that the Pope's great enemy—Colonna by name—struck the old pontiff in the face with his fist. It is known that the two messengers of the king heaped great indignities upon the Pope. They, the French, were driven out of the community but the humiliation caused by the indignities suffered by the Pope caused the death of Boniface VIII.

With the idea of condemning Boniface VIII, even after his death, and shielding himself from ecclesiastical censure, Philip ignored Benedict XI, and caused the Archbishop of Bordeaux, a French prelate, to be made Pope under the name of Clement V. It was agreed between the French Pope and Philip that the former would subordinate himself to the King, which considerably reduced the moral influence of the Church in other parts of Europe.

Clement V was crowned at Lyons in 1305 and in 1309 he established himself at Avignon, a possession of the Holy See on the then border of France. From 1309 to 1376 there followed seven French Popes. That particular period is known as the Babylonian captivity in church history.

In the year 1283 Wales was conquered by England under Edward I. The king gave to his eldest son the title of "Prince of Wales." Since that time the eldest son of all English Monarchs has had that title.

In 1337 the longest war recorded in history was started between England and France. It is known as the Hundred Years War because it lasted, with only a few short intermissions, one hundred years. The French coveted the territory controlled by England around Bordeaux. England would not allow the towns of Ghent and Bruges, which were their best customers for wool, to pass to the French. Edward III claimed the French throne because of the fact that his mother was the sister of the last French king. Philip VI, then reigning in France, was the previous French king's cousin. When Philip V became king of France, in 1316, it was decreed that no female should succeed to the throne of France. That decree was known, or thought to be a part of the Salic Law. Underlying the determination on the part of the French not to be ruled from England or by an Englishman, France invoked the Salic Law which prohibited the right of inheritance on the part of Edward's mother.

To go into all of the details of the Hundred Years War is useless insofar as the intent of this outline is concerned. However, it is necessary to deal with some detail in order to bring out the results as they affect the nationalistic spirit which is now in the ascendent. Accompanied by the nationalistic spirit was the development on a larger scale than heretofore ever known, government by representation. We have noted that in France the States General was called into existence under Philip IV. In England, under Edward I, the king, against his wishes, swore to the "Confirmation of the Charters" which prevented taxation without the consent of

Parliament. It is also worth noting that under Edward I, the king yielded to popular demand and banished the Jews who were permitted to take their property from the kingdom.

In 1337 Edward III entered France and publicly made his claim to the throne of France. The first battle was at sea near Fort Sluys (1340). Thirty thousand Frenchmen were drowned or killed in that battle. That naval engagement established Britain as mistress of the sea.

In Brittany there arose a disputed succession whereby the Salic Law again became involved, this time being on the British side. In order to settle that dispute hostilities were renewed in 1341. The war consisted of sieges on fortresses and towns and was continued for twenty-four years. Edward gained an overwhelming victory at Crecy in 1346, after having been attacked with imprudent haste by the French who faced the English with a powerful army. It was during that battle that an old maxim was coined. The English King's eldest son, who was known as the Black Prince, was hard pressed and called upon his father for aid. But the King refused him the assistance requested, saying "Let the boy win his spurs". Scotland who had allied itself with France was also defeated under the leadership of David Bruce. Bruce was made prisoner; the French were prostrated in Brittany. A ten month truce was concluded between kings.

Inasmuch as social conditions are as important as a matter of historical record, it is worth mentioning here that in 1347 a great pestilence swept over Europe. It was known as the "Black Death". Finding its source in Egypt or further east it passed through Italy to Paris spreading great destruction in its wake. In England one-half of the population is said to have perished. By 1349 it had practically worn itself out.

The defeat at Crecy so reduced the power of France that at times the kingdom was almost extinct. The king, however, acquired Montpellier from James of Aragon and the Dauphine of Vienne by purchase from the Dauphin,

Humbert II, who entered a monastery. From that time the title Dauphin was given to the heir to the French crown.

Philip VI was succeeded to the throne of France by John II of Normandy, called "the Good." Paradoxical as it may appear, John was a gay, extravagant, passionate and cruel king. His dealings with the king of Navarre, Charles "The Bad", who was considered a better man than John caused the English to obtain an ally on French soil and brought great disaster to France. John refused him promised fiefs and threw him into prison. His brother Philip of Navarre joined the English against John in Normandy. The "Black Prince" of England ravaged the provinces around Guienne. In 1356 a great battle took place at Potiers. John advanced upon the English prince with vastly superior numbers. The French made the same blunder that was made by them under Philip at Crecy. The attack was made by King John with so much impetuosity and rashness that he was completely defeated, with eleven thousand dead on the field of battle. John, and most of the nobility, were taken prisoners. While John was treated with great courtesy by the English, after his defeat and capture, the peasantry suffered tremendously.

The reaction of this last defeat caused an insurrection in Paris which brought the middle classes to the fore. While John was a prisoner in England, France was under the leadership of the Dauphin who took his orders from the States General at the instigation of the middle classes. The reaction gave birth to another reaction toward the royal cause which was productive of a civil war. Marcel, provost of traders (head of the municipality of Paris), lead against the latest reaction, but the Dauphin got the upper hand. Marcel was assassinated, the movement toward a free parliamentary government fell. Had Marcel been victorious it no doubt would have changed the course of events in France which culminated in 1793 in the great and bloody French Revolution.

In 1360 the captive King John made a treaty with Edward III, giving the English king one-half of his dominions.

That treaty was repudiated by the Dauphin. Edward thereupon invaded France with an immense force, but Charles wisely avoided an engagement. A new peace was concluded whereby Aquitaine, with several other lordships, was ceded to Edward and Edward, in turn, renounced all claim to the French crown, Normandy, and to all other former possessions of the Plantagenets, north of the Loire. The king was set at liberty by the payment of the first installment of his ransom. King John left one of his sons in England as a hostage, to secure the English against the non-payment of the future installments of his ransom. The son fled, thereupon John returned to England. The usual courtesy was extended to him, but he died soon thereafter.

Charles V (the Wise) succeeded to the throne of France and undertook the task of restoring the economic situation to normalcy. The Burghers (middle class) had been sorely grieved by the debasement of the coin. The king successfully restored the value of the coin. The king of Navarre (Charles) was subdued and the throne of Castile, over which there was bitter strife between Henry of Transtamara and Peter the Cruel, his half-brother, was the next matter to be settled before again resuming hostilities against England on a large scale. The Black Prince of England supported Peter. In 1369, with the support of Charles and the hero of the day—Du-Guesclin, a gentleman of Brittany who led the armies in Spain, Henry was established on the throne of Castile. That success delivered France from the great companies of Freebooters which previously had been running rampart over the kingdom. The entire internal administration of the kingdom having been reformed, Charles felt himself strong enough to continue the conflict with England.

Another advantage that Charles enjoyed was that the Aquitanian subjects were dissatisfied with the English. It appears that the dissatisfaction resulted largely because of the supercilious ways of the English.

Charles declared war (1369), and the English landed at Calais. Edward III was old and the Black Prince was ill.

The French army, under the leadership of the Duke of Burgundy, refused to meet the English. The following year the situation repeated itself. The French, under the Duke of Anjou, reconquered most of the Aquitanian territory. Du Guesclin was made constable of the French army, having been placed above the nobles by birth. He drove the Duke of Montfort out of Brittany. The English fleet was destroyed before Rochelle in 1372, by Castilian ships of war. The result of those misfortunes of the English was that a truce was entered into (1375). In 1377 Edward III died, whereupon Charles renewed the war and succeeded in capturing or winning back practically all English possessions in France. After one last cruel exploit in France, the sacking of Limoges in 1370, the Black Prince returned to England, broken in health.

The death of the Black Prince was deplored in England because he did much to save the country from misrule, while his father the king was old and feeble.

At this period Parliament was exercising its powers and making itself felt in England. The King's ministers were for the first time impeached by parliament. The manufacture of fine woolen cloths in England began during the reign of Edward III, at whose insistence Flemish weavers were imported into England.

During the reign of Edward III John Wickliffe became prominent. In 1366 Pope Urban V demanded payment of the arrears under the agreement entered into by King John and Rome, which has been heretofore referred to. Parliament refused payment on the ground that the kingdom could not be subjected to a foreigner. Wickliffe supported the king against the demands of the Pope. The Mendicant orders were growing very strong at this time and came into conflict with the secular clergy. Wickliffe supported the parish or secular clergy. He also contended that the clergy possessed too much wealth and power. His was the first translation of the Bible into English. His followers were nicknamed Lollards (psalm singers).

The son of the Black Prince succeeded to the throne of England (1377). Richard II had to deal with a great insurrection four years after his accession. It is worth noting that the first leader of the insurrection in Essex was a priest, who assumed the name of Jack Straw. At Blackheath the insurgents numbered one hundred thousand men. John Ball, a priest, worked the mob up to a furor demanding equality of rights, using the text:

"When Adam delved and Eve span,
Who was then a gentleman?"

Richard subdued the insurrection by making promises. In 1399 Richard was forced to resign the crown. Parliament deposed him in the name of misgovernment and, not long after, he was murdered. The Duke of Lancaster, who was the son of John of Gaunt, was made king under the name of Henry the Fourth. Under Richard the statute of praemunire of 1353 was renewed. That statute imposed harsh penalties upon anyone procuring excommunications or sentences against the king or realm.

Henry IV ascended the throne in 1399. The outstanding events of his reign were the putting down of two rebellions, one against the Welsh, another was that of the Northumberland family of the Persys, undertaken in behalf of the former king if he were alive. Henry died while praying at the Shrine of St. Edward in Westminster. In that reign heretics were growing in numbers and proceedings against them were severe. Parliament was inclined to be easy in the enforcement of the law against heresy because of the fact that a great amount of jealousy existed between that body and the clergy.

Charles VI, at the age of twelve, succeeded to the throne of France in 1380. As a result of a conquest over the regency two factions came into being, the Burgundians and the Armagnacs. The king became insane, resulting in a bitter contest for power between the factions. Those were the days of the great papal schism, and while the Burgundians of the north adhered to the Pope at Rome, Urban VI, the Armagnacs allied themselves with the French Pope Clement VII.

Henry V (1413-1422) was ruling in England and was having considerable difficulty with his nobles who were scheming to bring about a rebellion. With the idea in mind of diverting their plans, he made certain demands upon France which were refused. He thereupon renewed the old claim of his great grandfather (Edward III) to the throne of France. With fifty thousand men he invaded France (1415). It should be noted that gunpowder was coming into use at that time, it having been first introduced during the latter part of the fourteenth century. However, bowmen were still a potential factor in warfare. After a terrible siege at Harfluer, in which thousands of his troops perished with sickness, Henry with nine thousand men marched toward Calais. He was confronted by the forces of the House of Orleans (Armagnacs), fifty thousand men or more (1415). The French were defeated, with eleven thousand men lost. It was another case of English infantry, with expert bowmanship, against the French cavaliers whose horses floundered in the mud. After this great French defeat, the factions' (Burgundians and Orleanians) fury became more bitter. The Burgundians allied themselves with the English and by the terms of the Treaty of Troyes (1420) the daughter of Charles VI was given in marriage to Henry V. Subject to the death of the insane king of France, Henry was made heir to the French throne, but was immediately made regent.

In 1422 both Henry V and Charles VI (the insane king) died. A regency was established for the infant king, Henry VI. The Armagnacs proclaimed Charles VII king, south of the River Loire. With the kingdom divided the national cause was again at a very low ebb. Just at that time fate decreed that a deliverer should arise to bring order out of Chaos. Jeanne D'arc (Joan of Arc), a pure, simple-hearted and highly religious maiden from Domremy, seventeen years of age, having heard of the suffering, felt that Heaven called her to liberate France. The contagiousness of her faith spread to others. She was commissioned by Charles, and on horse, with banner in hand, joined the French soldiers. Inspired by her, the forces under Charles forced the English to give up the siege of Orleans, which was followed by other English defeats. Jeanne was known as the Maid of Orleans. She escorted Charles to Rheims and stood with him at his coronation. The Burgundians finally captured her before Paris and turned her over to the English who were allied with them. After being subjected to grievous indignities, she was condemned as a witch and burned at the stake at Rouen (1431). A great historian says of her, "The last word she uttered was 'Jesus'". Her character was without a taint. In her soul the spirit of religion and of patriotism burned with a pure flame; a heroine and a saint combined. She died "a victim to the ingratitude of her friends and the brutality of her foes."

A friendly understanding was arrived at in 1435, between the Duke of Burgundy and Charles VII which brought about unity within the kingdom. In 1449 the war was again renewed. The contest of a century came to an end in 1453 when the English were badly defeated.

With the exception of averting various rebellions on the part of the nobles and sometimes the masses, the English kings gained little by their constant warfare with France, and indeed lost much. England held only Calais, Harvre, and Guines Castle.

France was desolated. What were once fertile fields, the territory was reduced to desert land, roamed only by wolves and bands of robbers.

In the year 1250 Frederick II of Germany died. Until his death the imperial authority extended over Germany and Italy. Subsequently for a period of twenty-three years, known as the "Great Interregnum", the two countries were left free from that authority. During that interim German cities grew strong, along with the Burghers of France, and the towns of England. However, there were many disturbances in Germany and the demand for local independence undermined the imperial idea to such an extent that the Empire never regained its former vigor. It was during the period of the

Interregnum that Denmark, Poland, Hungary and other vassals of the Holy Roman Empire broke away from it.

The beginning of the House of Hapsburg, which in modern times has influenced world affairs considerably, came when Rudolph, Count of Hapsburg (1273-1291) was elected emperor of the Holy Roman Empire. Rudolph made no attempt to rule in Italy. He was friendly and submissive to the Pope and confined himself chiefly to putting down disorders in Germany and compelling the King of Bohemia who held Austria, Styria, and Carniola to recognize him as Emperor of the Holy Roman Empire. He defeated Ottocar II, king of Bohemia, in a great battle at Marchfield in 1278, and the latter's possessions fell into the Emperor's hands. That victory laid the foundation of the power of the House of Hapsburg.

Switzerland was originally part of the kingdom of Arles. From the year 1033 it was part of the Empire. Zurich, Basel, Berne, and Freiburg became important factors in trade and gained considerable municipal privileges. Early in the thirteenth century the Counts of Hapsburg exercised some jurisdiction over the country and endeavored to get absolute control. Two of the Swiss districts came into the Empire, but after the death of Rudolph, the three districts, which for a long time were imbued with the spirit of freedom, united. After much fighting with the Austrians, which in every instance resulted in the defeat of the latter, the Swiss Confederacy was organized. From the year 1388 Switzerland has been self-ruling.

During the period of the Babylonian Captivity Italy was left without the influence of the Pope and imperial control. Two distinct factions sprung up, namely the Guelphs and the Ghibellines. The former represented the republican idea while the latter were imperialists. That development resulted in a series of civil wars extending through the cities of Florence, Genoa, Naples, Venice, etc. It was during that period that Dante produced his immortal poem which was inspired by the sufferings which he beheld and which took hold of his innermost feelings. Dante was of noble birth, but not of the highest rank. He was by far the most learned, insofar as literature was concerned, of his time, having received the teachings of the best masters of the day. It is said that no poet before exceeded him in depth of thought and feeling. His family represented the republican cause, as did he in the early part of his career, but the force of circumstances placed him into the imperial ranks during the latter part of his life.

The Guelfs and republicanism finally triumphed in Florence (1253). Citizenship was confined to those who had enrolled themselves in the guilds, therefore the nobles were excluded from government. The latter, therefore, dropped their titles in order to enroll in the guilds.

Later what was known as the feuds of the Guelph factions sprang up. That was a difference between the Blacks and the Whites. Then strife broke out between the craftsmen; the Lesser Arts, and the Greater Arts (14th century).

The net result of the disturbances was to reduce all classes to one level and opened the way for families of wealth to gain control of government.

The political result of the various civil wars and disturbances in the middle of fifteenth century Italy, was that we find surviving out of the chaos, the kingdom of Naples, duchy of Milan, republics of Florence and Venice and the principality of the Pope. The Visconti family were the leaders in Milan. Venice was under constitutional government. The Medici family was prominent in Florence and had practical control of the government.   In Rome, during the Papal schism, as was also the case in other cities, towns and territories were ceded to nobles as fiefs, and it was not until Pope Nicholas V and his successors came along, after the great schism of the Church, that the fragments of the Papal territory were unified.

Dante and his contemporaries were followed by an era of culture, embracing the study of the arts. Venice and Pisa led in the trend of culture, as was exemplified by the building of the Church of St. Marks in Byzantine style at Venice in 1071 and the leaning tower at Piza in the twelfth century.

The interior cities flourished with manufacture while the seaports of Venice and Genoa were main arteries of commerce to the far east, Spain, and France. It is interesting to note that the Italians were the world's first bankers. In 1171 the Bank of Venice was founded and in 1407 the Bank of Genoa. It is said that during that era of advance civilization in Italy, the most important elements lacking were the low tone of patriotism and morality, the latter having sunk to very low levels.

In this outline we have left Spain since the time that the Frank infantry stopped the Arabs, or the Saracens, at the Pyrenees. Out of the minor kingdoms of Leon and Asturia, and still other kingdoms, grew Castile. Castile to Spain was what France was to Gaul. Portugal became a kingdom in 1139. Now we find Portugal on the Atlantic coast, Aragon on the Mediterranean and the big power Castile spread to the interior.

The Moslems still retained Grenada in the South. Castile and Aragon in 1492 captured the Moslem kingdom of Grenada. The respective monarchs of Castile and Aragon, Ferdinand and Isabella were united in marriage and the kingdoms were united in 1506.

An interesting development in government is to be noted in the constitutions of the erstwhile kingdoms of Castile and Aragon. In Aragon the Cortes, which was the general assembly restricted the kings in their authority. The assembly was composed of all classes of nobles, the clergy and deputies from the cities. The Cortes reserved the right to make laws and pass on taxation. The king could not pass judgment on any member of the Cortes without the warrant of the highest judicial officer. In the event of the violation of the latter restriction, the Cortes were vested with the right to elect another king. In Castile, from the year 1169, the deputies from the cities were admitted to the Cortes. The power of the cities became greater than that of the nobles and the clergy, but upon the accession of Henry of Trastámara the nobles' power became greater than that of the king.

Early in the fifteenth century the people of Castile were possessed of more power, compared with the king, relatively than the people of any country in Europe. However, the representation of the people came through the deputies of the cities. The nearest approach to Castile was in England, where representation was made through the landed proprietors.

In Aragon extraordinary authority was vested in the justiciary, or justice, by its constitution. Barcelona united with Aragon and was a great seat of commerce. The first code of maritime law was framed and written at Barcelona. Personal rights were asserted very vehemently against any encroachments by the kings.

Up to the fifteenth century Portugal, which became a kingdom in 1185, was busy fighting the Moors, the African Mohammedans, which had invaded Spain and Portugal at intervals. Madeira was discovered by the Portuguese in 1419. In 1432 Portugal occupied the Azores.

The Scandinavian countries, up to the early part of the middle ages, stand out only because of their piratical expeditions which were to influence Europe to a great degree in its future development. We have already read of the activities of the Northmen in France, whose industry and sturdiness turned forests into fertile fields. The Scandinavian peninsulas consisted of Denmark, Norway and Sweden. The peninsula never came under the influence of the early Roman Empire nor the Holy Roman Empire. The same is true of the larger part of Great Britain and all of Spain. The peninsula was converted to Christianity, as has been heretofore recorded, during the tenth and eleventh centuries. After the introduction of the teachings of Christ, piracy ceased, and these countries joined with the rest of Europe in its march toward a higher civilization. The countries had to go through their period of chaos in shaping themselves into individualities. The usual wars, kings, excommunications, differences between nobles and the kings took place. In addition to the wars and general chaos which was in evidence during the centuries, these countries were united and disunited at various times.

In Poland, up to 1370, a dynasty known as the Piast Dynasty was in power. Boleslav I, in 992, was crowned king by his bishops. He was excommunicated by Pope Gregory VII. Up to 1370 Poland was an important kingdom, having had to fight its way to individuality in the usual method. Casimir III, by his defeat of the Russians, carried its boundaries to the Dnieper. Casimir gave great impulse to commerce and framed a code of laws for the country. It is said that every man who was able to own and equip a horse was counted as a noble. The election of every king, according to the political constitution, had to be sanctioned by the nobles who alone made up the diet. The peasants were the chief tax-payers.

Under Rurik the Northmen settled in Russia. They pushed their conquests to the south from Novgorod; centuries later Kiev, on the Dnieper, became their capital. Vladimir I was converted to Greek Christianity in the year 980. They were quite powerful up to 1051. The custom of the sovereigns was to divide their dominions among their sons, which resulted in cutting the country up into small principalities which, in turn, resulted in fierce contests among themselves. While engaged in these resultless and bloody contests of the Mongols (Asiatic Tribes) became their great invasion of Russia. The "Golden Horde", which the Mongols established on the Volga, held the Russians in their vise for two centuries. At the time of the Mongol invasion Novgorod was still the capital. Moscow became the capital at the end of the thirteenth century. Muscovy, derived from the name Moscow, was to be to Russia what France in the days of Rome was to be to the modern France. Lithuania and Poland were absorbing by conquest the early or western Russia; and, while those conquests were taking place, Moscow was building up the Russia of the east which gave birth to modern Russia.

The founder of the Russian monarchy was Ivan I, in 1328. Ivan made Moscow his capital. In 1382 the Mongols burned Moscow and twenty-four thousand of its inhabitants were slaughtered. During the reign of Ivan III (the Great) 1462-1505, the Russians were delivered entirely from the control of the Mongols.

In order to avoid the Mongols, the Ottoman Turks, at the end of the thirteenth century, shifted their activities from the region of the Caspian Sea and conquered the kingdom of Seljukians, in Asia Minor. Osman (Ottoman), advanced into Greek territory, capturing cities of importance and wealth in his path. The Byzantine court could not make an effective resistance because of the fact that the empire had worn itself out. Adrianople was taken by the Turks and was made the seat of authority (1361-1363). Ancient cities, founded by the Romans and Greeks, were overrun. Murad I was slain in the battle of Kosovo where the Serbians and Bulgarians made a stand against the fierce onslaughts of the Turks. Bajazet, son of Murad, came into power after the latter's death. Macedonia, Thessaly, and Greece came into his possession. In 1396 Emperor Sigismund and John of Burgundy, with one hundred thousand men were defeated at Nicopolis. The emperor escaped by sea, ten thousand prisoners were slaughtered and a large ransom redeemed French counts and knights. Bosnia came into the possession of Bajazet. The seat of the Byzantine government, Constantinople, had to pay tribute. The latter city was saved from the Turks at this time only because of Bajazet's fear of the oncoming Mongolian invasion.

Timur (Tamerlane), a descendant of Genghis Khan, who had previously conquered China, the northern part of Asia and sacked practically all of Europe with his Tartars, had revived the Tarter kingdom.

He rapidly made himself master from the Chinese wall to the Mediterranean and from Egypt to Moscow. His march was a repetition of his conquering ancestor, destroying civilization and marking it with blood. At Ispahan, in

Persia, he killed seventy thousand persons, and at Delhi one hundred thousand prisoners of war were slaughtered. It is said that he delighted in building pyramids of heads before city gates. In 1401, at Bagdad, he piled up ninety thousand heads. He got as far as Moscow in Russia. Then came a test of strength between Bajazet and his Turks and Tamerlane. On June 16th, 1402 four hundred thousand Turks and eight hundred thousand Mongols met in combat at Ancyra. The Turks were defeated and Bajazet was taken prisoner. When Bajazet was taken before Tamerlane the Mongol leader was playing chess with his son. Asia Minor came into Tamerlane's hands. Bajazet died soon after that defeat, Tamerlane died in 1405.

Tamerlane's Empire soon dissolved. Murad II, the grandson of Bajazet, entered into the field of conquest. The Byzantine Empire was completely surrounded by the power of the Turks. Constantinople and a small amount of adjacent territory was all that remained of the Byzantine. From the time of the Greek Schism from the Roman

Church, many attempts had been made by Byzantine emperors to bring about a union. All had failed chiefly because of doctrinal interpretations. Now that the eastern empire was in great danger of the oncoming Turks another effort was made by John VII, Byzantine Emperor. He went to Italy, with many bishops, and after many drawn out conferences, a verbal agreement was arrived at with Rome. All of the effort was in vain, however, because of the disfavor that the agreement met with in Constantinople.

Mohammed II succeeded Murad II in 1451. He was determined that Constantinople was to be his capital. At this time Constantine XII was the Byzantine Emperor. He worshipped in accordance with the Roman rites, while his court worshipped according to the Greek Church. Mohammed made his anticipated attack on the capital which was defended by seven thousand men. After a siege of fifty-three days, Constantinople fell before the furious assaults of the Turks. It is said that Constantine cast off his golden armor and fell in battle bravely fighting with the defenders on May 29, 1453.

Some of the significant changes brought about by the ceaseless warfare during the middle ages, were: the establishment of universities followed by the higher education of the middle classes; the centralizing of governmental authority by the subjection of the lords to the authority of the kings; the increased right of suffrage of the serfs, with increased power and self-respect of the middle classes; reduced superiority of the knights, due to the invention of gunpowder, which made the peasants as powerful a foe as the mounted knight; and the lessening of the power of the church, caused by the lack of unity among church leaders.

Inasmuch as the church is so interwoven with the history of universal politics from the time of Constantine the Great, the reader will doubtless pause to ask, what is the history of the "Great Schism" of 1054, which separated the Eastern Greek Orthodox from the Western Roman Catholic Church, about which volumes could be written and have been; therefore, it must be understood that the subject is beyond the range of this outline. But here we come to what is known as the Western Schism, or the Great Occidental Schism of 1378, a period which had its beginnings with what is known as "The Babylonian Exile," which began in 1309, after a severe disagreement between Philip the Fair of France and Pope Boniface VIII, and lasted over a period of seventy years.

We have read that Pope Boniface died over the humiliation inflicted upon him by the emissaries of Philip. Benedict XII followed Boniface, but died nine months after his accession. Through Philip's influence a French prelate, the Archbishop of Bordeaux, Clement V was made Pope. Clement was crowned at Lyons in 1305 and in 1309 made the pontifical headquarters at Avignon.

Gregory XI, who held the pontifical authority from 1370-1378, put an end to the Popedom in Avignon. The people of many papal cities in Italy were making efforts to throw off their allegiance to the Pope. Gregory decided that the only way to prevent a schism was for the Pope to reside in Rome. He therefore returned to Rome where his presence brought great joy to all good Christians. Rome, however, was not an altogether safe place for him and, thinking his life in danger, issued a special bull which empowered the sixteen cardinals who accompanied him to Rome, to at once elect his successor by a simple majority without a conclave or awaiting the arrival of those cardinals that remained at Avignon. Upon the death of Gregory XI the Romans feared the restoration of the See of Avignon. They also feared the election of another French Pope. The sixteen cardinals called a conclave where the Romans insisted upon either a Roman or an Italian to be made Pope. The Archbishop of Bari (Urban VI), was elected by the cardinals. A subsequent election was held with all the cardinals voting. The second election confirmed the first and by virtue of documents addressed to bishops throughout Christendom, their assistance at his coronation and the homage paid him, removed all doubt of the legitimacy of Urban's election.

However, the French cardinals rancored under the inflexibility of the new Pontiff and spread the propaganda to the effect that Urban's election was made under compulsion and was therefore invalid. Under the leadership and inspiration of the French cardinals, eleven in all, they retired to Anagni, declared the Holy See vacant and elected Cardinal Robert of Genova (Clement VII). Fearing for his safety in Italy, Clement took up his residence at Avignon.

Thus began what is known as the "Great Schism of the West", which was destined to last thirty-nine years and which brought great sorrow to all well-meaning Christians of the time (1378-1417).

France, Naples, Aragon, Castile and Scotland adhered to Clement. The balance of Italy, Germany, England, Hungary, Portugal and the Scandinavian kingdoms acknowledged Urban.

The hopes of Clement and his cardinals were dashed to pieces when the Italian cardinals refused to recognize him, upon the death of Urban. They proceeded to elect Peter Tomacelli (Boniface IX) 1389-1404.

The University of Paris, which was the center of theology, became very prominent in its efforts to put an end to the existing state of affairs, suggesting three methods of settlement: resignation of the two pontiffs, arbitration by impartial judges, or the convocation of a general council. At the same time a letter was addressed by the university to Clement VII by which he was so affected that he was seized with a sudden illness which caused his death (1394). Upon his death, and fearing the Sorbonne (University of Paris), the cardinals at Avignon hastened to elect Peter de Luna, who was famous for his craftiness. Peter de Luna took the title of Benedict XIII. Before his election he was pledged under oath that he would do everything in his power to end the schism, to the extent of resigning all claims to the Papacy, if necessary. Peter de Luna, it is fairly safe to conclude, became a potential factor in the prolongation of the schism. He absolutely refused to resign his high office, when called upon to keep his word upon many occasions, and especially when the French national assembly at Paris, in 1395, demanded his withdrawal. His extreme adroitness was shown when he succeeded in bringing over to his side Nicholas de Clémanges, the learned rector of the Sorbonne, along with St. Vincent Ferrer, the thaumaturgus of the age, and Peter d'Ailly, the greatest theologian of the day, who accepted a bishopric from him.

In 1398 another national assembly was held, at which France withdrew its obedience from Benedict (de Luna). Abandoned by all of his cardinals, except two, for five years he was kept a prisoner at Avignon. However, his adroitness came to the fore once more when he effected his escape and succeeded in gaining popular favor again in France, which was followed by France returning to his obedience.

In the meantime the King Wenceslaus of Germany and King Richard II of England demanded that Pope Boniface resign and were preparing to use force, when both princes were deposed by events in their respective kingdoms.

In 1404 Innocent VII succeeded Boniface IX. The revolt of the Romans and his death prevented him from carrying out his plan for the convocation of a general council for the purpose of bringing the schism to an end.

Prior to the election of a successor to Innocent VII, all Roman cardinals singly pledged themselves under oath that whomsoever among them was elected, one would resign the pontifical office just as soon as the Avignonese Pope abdicated or died. That election made Gregory XIII (1406-1416) a man of sterling virtue, the Roman Pope. A meeting between the two Popes was arranged to take place at Savona, in 1407. Gregory had already expressed a willingness to resign, if Benedict would do the same. Benedict appeared at the appointed place under a strong guard. Gregory, fearing for the safety of his person and not without reason, failed to appear. The latter failure was a great disappointment to all those Christian people whose hearts had been gladdened by the thought of a possible settlement of the differences within the church at Savona.

The hopes of both obediences having once more been dashed to pieces, the cardinals of both parties abandoned their respective Pope and called for a Council at Pisa. Gregory objected vehemently to the council at Pisa on the ground that the right of convoking a General Council belonged to the Pope. He signified his willingness to convoke a General Council at some place other than Pisa, but stood firm on his refusal to attend the latter council, which he claimed he could not do without degrading the pontifical authority. The greater part of Christendom, however, followed the cardinals and renounced its obedience to Gregory. The council met in 1409 at Pisa and was under the presidency of Guido de Malésec, senior cardinal.

The attendance consisted of twenty-four cardinals from both obediences, four patriarchs, two hundred archbishops and bishops, a great number of generals of orders, abbots, doctors, deputies of universities and the ambassadors of nearly all of the European sovereigns. The council cited both Pontiffs to appear before it and it was decreed that their failure to appear should cause all good Christians to renounce them. The council proceeded to depose both Popes on the ground that they were contumacious and schismatical, and declared the Holy See to be vacant. Then it was ordained that a conclave be held. Thereupon Cardinal Philargi was made Pope Alexander V.

After the adjournment of the Council of Pisa, and much to the surprise and chagrin of the Church, the latter discovered that now, instead of two Popes to deal with, it had three. Naples with some cities in Italy, King Rupprecht of Germany, but not the German Empire, remained true to Gregory.   Aragon,

Castile, Sardinia, and Scotland supported Benedict, while Alexander was recognized by the rest of Christendom.

After having the Pontificate only ten months, Alexander was succeeded by John XXIII. In 1412 John convened a council at Rome, which was a fulfillment of a resolution made at Pisa. The council was very poorly attended and not much was accomplished. After condemning the dogmas of Wycliffe and John Huss, both of whom had stirred up considerable doctrinal agitation, the council adjourned.

Sigismund was Emperor of the Holy Roman Empire at this time. Rome was invaded by King Ladislaus and John XXIII was compelled to seek protection from the emperor. The latter demanded that the Pope (John) convoke a general council in some German city for the purpose of terminating the schism. Therefore, in November 1414, a Council was called at Constance, with a three-fold purpose: extinguishing the schism, reforming the church in its Head as well as its Members, and of extirpating heresy.

The Council was opened by Pope John personally and was attended by about eighteen thousand ecclesiastics of all ranks. This council agreed, against the wishes of Pope John, that it was independent of the Council of Pisa and that representatives of the Popes Gregory and Benedict would be received as papal legates. To offset the great majority of Italian votes, which composed about one-half of the total and who almost to a man supported Pope John, it was agreed that the right of suffrage was to extend to abbots, chapters, deputies of universities, doctors and ambassadors of nations, that the voting was to be by nations and not by individuals. The nations were: 1st the Italians; 2nd French; 3rd the Germans, Poles and Scandinavians; and 4th the English. The Spaniards had net yet joined the council, but were later added. In 1417 the Council proclaimed Martin V Pope and the cleft in the Rock was closed.